# ENTREPRENEAL$™
# WORKBOOK OF BUSINESS

COPYRIGHT © 2020

Published by: SMS Write On Publishing, Buffalo New York
Cover and Information Design by Rita Neal, MBA
Editor: Shannon Spruill for SMS Write On Publishing

All rights reserved. No part of this book may be reproduced in any form without written permission from the publisher.

ISBN: 978-0-578-69188-6

Printed in the United States of America

## TABLE OF CONTENTS

3   TABLE OF CONTENTS

4   DEDICATION

5   FOREWARD

6   PREFACE

8   WHAT YOU WILL LEARN

9   INTRODUCTION

17   DESIGN THINKING

25   BUSINESS MODELS

26   ELEVATOR PITCH

28   BRAND & PROMOTIONS

38   PRICING

46   BUSINESS PLAN

60   REFERENCES

63   DEFINITIONS

65   ABOUT US

This book is dedicated to the dreamers and thinkers who believe in their ideas enough to make them real. To the entrepreneurs...

# FOREWARD

By Brodie Johnson, PhD
Pastor, Cornerstone Institutional Baptist Church
Director of Project Management at Dufresne Spencer Group, LLC

Rita was a student in a few of my business classes at Belhaven University. Went I met her as an undergraduate student, she and her husband had just started a business. When we met again during her graduate studies, she and her husband had closed that business and started another.

She contacted me in early 2020 to ask if I would write a foreward for this workbook. I was not surprised to learn that she and her husband were still in business and had recently formed a new Limited Liability Corporation. Rita was always astute and tenacious in her studies, so I expected to hear nothing less.

This workbook is super. Rita presents outstanding detail and content from beginning to end. I was very intrigued by the 16 Personalities Test and Entrepreneur Assessment Questionnaire and quite surprised by my results.

This book is designed for anyone that has an interest in starting their own business. Rita presents the information in a way that holds your attention. Her meticulous efforts will assist those who have an interest in entrepreneurship, even those who have started a business and need more insight into the path they have chosen.

This workbook is easy to read with guided, interactive exercises that help prepare the reader for the work involved when starting a business. It is a must-have and I daresay, a necessary point of reference for anyone considering entrepreneurship as a means to supplement or replace employment income.

Congratulations on a superb job!

Brodie Johnson, PhD.

# PREFACE

You may be at an entrepreneurial workshop, in a classroom or, you may have ordered this workbook online. No matter where you are or who you are, I know three things about you - you want more for yourself; you want to contribute something to the world that will make it a better place; you are a dreamer and thinker, ready to create your own opportunity. You are one of the reasons I created this workbook series.

I earned my Master of Business Administration in 2019. I learned a lot about how to manage and run somebody else's business, not how to start my own. Reason 2: I wanted to create a comprehensive resource guide for others interested in entrepreneurship. I was fired from a job in 2013 after 11 years of helping maintain wealth for others. Reason 3: I wanted to use my time and talents to create income for *me* and *my family,* and teach them how to do the same.

Whatever your reasons for wanting to start a business, just know that entrepreneurship is hard. There is a lot of risk involved with little recognition or reward. I worked a full-time job, was a full time student AND worked full-time with my husband on our business. When I got frustrated or doubted if what I was doing provided value or would make a difference in the world; I just reminded myself of how it felt to be fired. That feeling fuels my passion for entrepreneurship and reinforces the truth of power in ownership.

In 2015, I helped my husband start our 3rd company with his vision and property management experience. We started out with five, generic, dollar store 'FOR RENT' signs. We wrote our contact numbers on them, and conducted business in parking lots - on the hoods of our cars. As Independent Leasing Agents, we provide a service to realtors and real estate investors. We exploited an industry need to create a niche service business that is becoming increasingly in demand.

# PREFACE

We had very limited resources then and still wear many hats as entrepreneurs now. I have learned: how to create a business plan, create websites and business pages on social media, the process for starting and registering a business, how to network, how to create legally binding contracts and so much more.

YOU can do the same thing; generate income using your God-given talents, your knowledge, and your passion. Working in your purpose will make the late nights and early mornings seem less like work. Be brave, be committed, be consistent

And now for the legal stuff:

Purchase and completion of the ENTREPRENEALS, LLC Workbook of Business does not guarantee any result or outcome. Individual results will vary and will depend solely on your capacity and willingness to learn, your business acumen, dedication, motivation and tenacity. By purchasing, you agree that ENTREPRENEALS LLC is not liable to you in any way for your results (or lack thereof) in using our products and/or services.

If advice concerning legal or related matters is needed, the services of a fully qualified professional should be sought. This workbook is not intended for use as a source of legal or business advice. You should be aware of any laws which govern business transactions or other business practices in your country and state.

# WHAT YOU WILL LEARN

- Understand the psychology behind business branding.

- Create a business name and logo around a product or service business.

- How to assess your personality for key traits needed to be a successful entrepreneur.

- Understand Design Thinking and how to use its processes to validate products, services and ideas.

- Map out a business model through activity based business planning.

- Understand how to price products or services.

- Assess skills and passions and apply them during ideation.

- Recognize and understand business models and the different types of entrepreneurs.

- Learn the components of a business plan.

- Fully articulate a business concept by creating an elevator pitch.

# WHAT IS AN ENTREPRENEUR

Someone who has an idea for a business and makes plans to create and run that business. Even though they may lose money, an entrepreneur is willing to take the risk to make a difference in their life and the lives of others.

## CHARACTERISTICS

- Visionary
- Passionate
- Adaptable
- Disciplined
- Risk taker
- Motivated
- Creative
- Persuasive
- Consistent
- Self-driven
- Focused
- Competitive
- Fearless
- Dynamic
- Proactive
- Thick skinned
- Innovative
- Perceptive
- Self-controlled
- Patient
- Articulate
- Confident

# WHICH TYPE OF ENTREPRENEUR ARE YOU?

## STARTUP ENTREPRENEUR

- Recognizes or creates an opportunity to make money
- Founds a company and takes all the risks
- Builds and grows their business fast
- Works many hours with little reward in the beginning

## LIFESTYLE ENTREPRENEUR

- Creates a business with the purpose of altering their personal lifestyle
- They want to focus on enjoying life without worrying about money
- Wants to put in very few hours of work with high income results

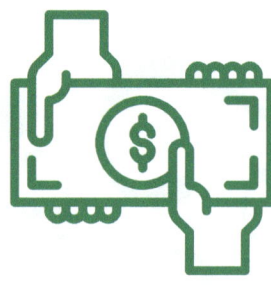

## SIDE HUSTLE ENTREPRENEUR

- They are both employed and self employed
- Low risk involved
- Work online, monetize a skill, flipping or wholesaling something

## SOCIAL ENTREPRENEUR

- A for profit business that supports social causes
- Solve social problems or effect social change through entrepreneurship

# TAKE THE 16 PERSONALITIES TEST

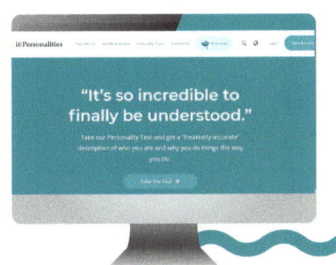

### 01 GO TO THE WEBSITE
http://www.16personalities.com/free-personality-test

### 02 TAKE THE TEST
Answer honestly to get the most accurate result.

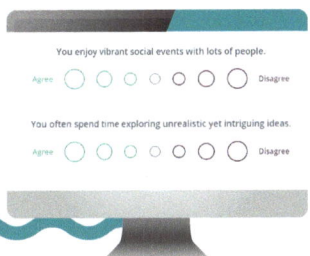

### 03 SURPRISED AT THE RESULTS?
How are they different from what you expected?

### 04 DO YOU AGREE WITH THE RESULTS?
If not, why not?

**WRITE YOUR 4 DIGIT CODE HERE**

# ENTREPRENEUR ASSESSMENT

## Answer each question honestly

Are you prepared to put in the hard work that is necessary to start and run a business?

_____
_____
_____

You won't always be motivated to work your business. Do you have the dicsipline to perservere through the setbacks?

_____
_____
_____

What has kept you from starting your business?

_____
_____
_____

How can you overcome this?

_____
_____
_____

# ENTREPRENEUR ASSESSMENT

## Answer each question honestly

What are you most passionate about? What do you absolutely love to do?

_____
_____
_____

What do you lose track of time doing? Can you potentially turn it into a business?

_____
_____
_____

Do people constantly ask for your help or advice?

_____
_____
_____

How would your life change if you were doing work that made you happy?

_____
_____
_____

# ENTREPRENEUR ASSESSMENT

## Answer each question honestly

What would your 'best life' look like? Write out the vision of your life.

_____
_____
_____
_____
_____
_____
_____
_____
_____
_____
_____
_____
_____
_____
_____

# ENTREPRENEUR ASSESSMENT

## Answer each question honestly

**Why is it so important to validate your business idea? How will you validate your business?**

_____
_____
_____

**If it seems like your business won't work, how will you pivot or adjust your product or service to make it more marketable?**

_____
_____
_____
_____
_____
_____
_____
_____

# Section 2

## TWO

# DESIGN THINKING

# WHAT IS DESIGN THINKING?

Design Thinking, as defined by Tim Brown, Executive Chair of Ideo, is: a human-centered approach to innovation that draws from the designer's toolkit to integrate the needs of people, the possibilities of technology, and the requirements for business success.

FYI - having the best product or service doesn't guarantee success. First time entrepreneurs will find it hard to cope with business situations which increase the likely hood of failure.

Design Thinking guides you through multi-level thinking that can help minimize the risks you take as a new entrepreneur starting a business.

It forces you to look outside what *you* think is great and focus on what the *consumer* or *user* thinks is great about your product or service.

# The data below is from the National Business Capital & Services Business Failure Rates and Startup Statistics for 2019

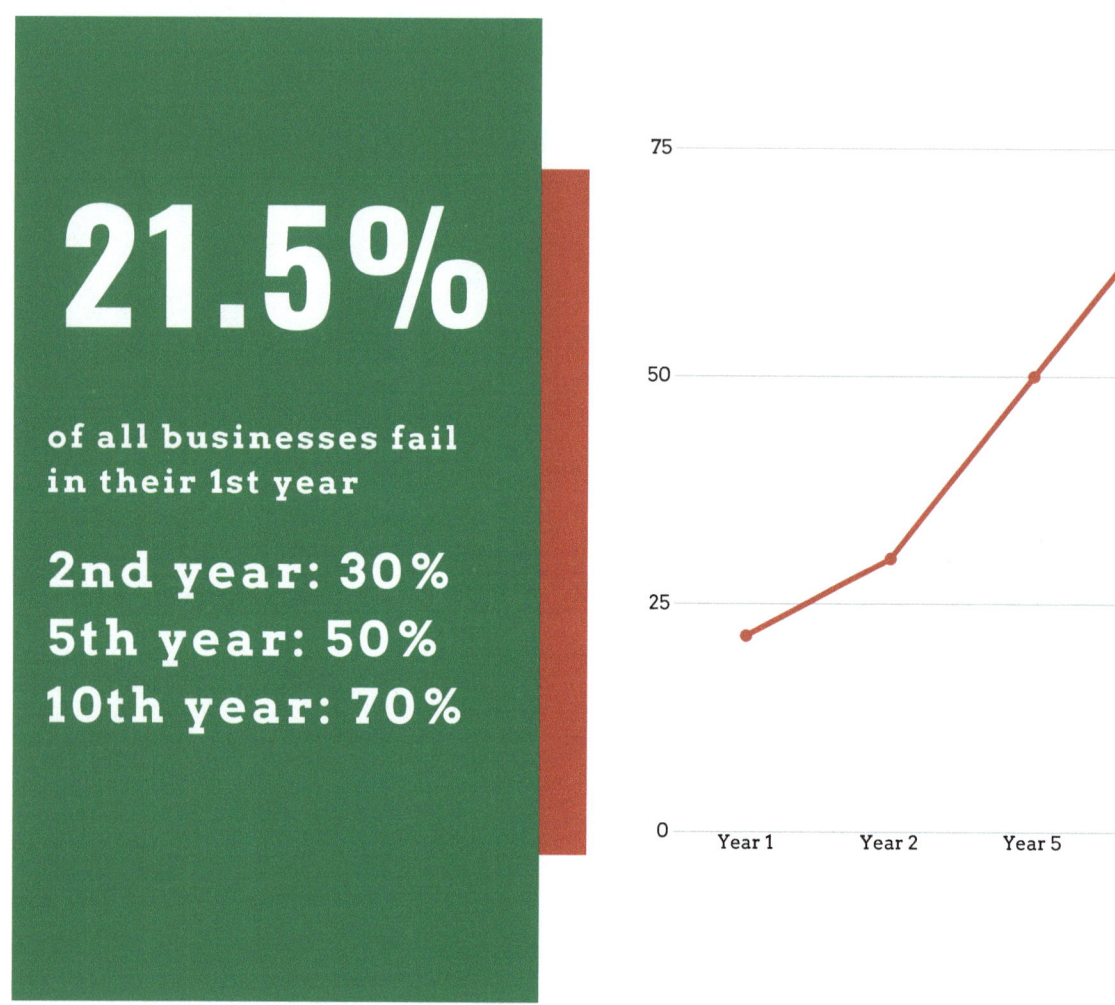

Some of the reasons businesses fail:

- started for the wrong reason
- don't differentiate themselves from their competition
- don't have enough cash flow
- don't know how to price their products and services
- don't understand their customer needs
- Poor leadership

Design Thinking allows business owners to focus on their customers while validating new business ideas, products or services, or improving old ones. The diagram on the next page shows how Design thinking is used to validate business ideas, products or services.

# DESIGN THINKING

**VALIDATION**

**EMPATHIZE**
- Understand users experience
- Interview or observe customer
- What does customer want and need

**DEFINE**
- Specific problem that prospective customers of your business are experiencing
- PAIN POINTS

**IDEATION**
- Form ideas. Imagine or conceive out of the box solutions
- BRAINSTORM

**PROTOTYPE**
- Mock ups, story boards least expensive and least amount of effort to produce
- MINIMUM VIABLE PRODUCT (MVP)

**TEST**
- Short cycle testing to improve design
- FAIL FORWARD

# Empathize

Understand who your customers (users) are and what they need. Ask survey questions to engage and connect. Pay attention to body language and facial expressions when they discuss or compare your product/service to others in the market. Be objective. Use any criticism to improve your product or service,

What does the user expect from your product or service?

**Age**

**Gender**

How do they compare your product/service to what's available?

**Income**

**Beliefs**

Why do they buy their current product or service and not others?

**Values**

**Lifestyle**

Does the user have suggestions on how to improve your product/service?

**Shop online or brick and mortar**

**Impulse or comparative shopper**

12

# Define

Define the user problem that you want to solve. Think from the user's point of view. Instead of: "I need to increase enrollment in my after school program by 30%", the statement should be based solely on the customer information gathered in the empathize phase: "Working parents need affordable options for after school care facilities that provide transportation so they don't have to leave work to pick kids up from school and drop them off at after school programs." Use this example and the prompts to the left, create or define your problem statement.

Who is experiencing the problem

What is the problem

Where is the problem happening (in home, where, online etc.)

Why do working parents need an after school program that provides trasportation,

What happens if parents leave work before their shift ends

How have parents handled transportation needs before now

How does not having after school transport affect parents work life and home life

How does solving the problem add value (to customer, to you)

# Ideation

Ideation is like brainstorming in the sense of generating ideas in a group setting. What you learned from the user in the Empathize stage helped you develop your problem statement in Define phase. You know who your customers are and the problem they need solved. There are several techniques used to generate ideas, but we will only focus on a few, Use the prompts to the left, to create or define your problem statement.

**Brainstorming**
Group comes up with different ideas to generate solutions

Brainwriting
Write ideas down and pass around to the group to add their ideas

**Brainwalking**
Say problem and solution. walk & stand next to someone who adds to or changes solution

**Analogies**
Compare problem to something you are familiar with to generate ideas

**Mindmapping**
Write a key word related to problem in the middle. s Draw lines out

**Reverse Thinking**
Visualize the user with product from purchase to consumption or use

**Storyboarding**
Visualize the user with product from purchase to consumption or use

**Worst Possible Idea**
naming the worst ideas helps think about ways to improve

# Prototype and Test

The solutions you came up with in the previous phase are used to create a prototype. You should create a minimum viable product - an inexpensive prototype that can be made to test with customers or friends to provide feedback for future development. If you're providing a service, think about the user experience before, during, and after services have been provided. Get feedback on what the customer didn't like or something they felt your service lacked.

Resources needed to test product or service?

Testing different variations of product or service?

How many users tested?

Where will testing be done?

What do users like least?

Changes need to be made?

Time frame from prototype to testing, improvement to final product?

Time frame from prototype to testing, improvement to final product?

TESTER 1

TESTER 2

TESTER 3

TESTER 4

# BUSINESS MODELS

Once you have validated your idea, product, or service and know which path of entrepreneurship is right for you, you can decide on your business model. Your business model is the plan for how your company will make money. It describes your product, your target marget, and your expenses.

# THE ELEVATOR PITCH

## WHAT IS AN ELEVATOR PITCH

An elevator pitch is a short 30 to 60 second presentation of your business idea, product or service to a customer or potential investor. If you're talking to a potential investor, highlight your business model, competitive advantage, and explain how it benefits them to invest in you. If you're talking to a potential customer highlight your eureka moment, how your product or service adds value to their lives and why they should choose you instead of your competition.

## INFO & TIPS

PRACTICE YOUR PITCH

TEST YOUR PITCH

SOLVE A PROBLEM

MAKE THEM ASK QUESTIONS

CALL TO ACTION

REJECTION IS OK

### PROBLEM
Talk about problem you defined in the Design Thinking process.

### SOLUTION
Talk about how your business proposes to solve it.

### EUREKA MOMENT
Talk briefly about the problem and how you were inspired to solve it.

### ASK A QUESTION
Ask an open ended question to engage your audience.

### COMPETITIVE ADVANTAGE
How will you set your business apart from the competition?

### BUSINESS MODEL
Touch on how your company will operate and make money.

### CALL TO ACTION
Leave a business card, sample product, offer free estimate of service, request meeting to present full business plan etc.

Always look the investor or customer in the eye. Give them a firm handshake and smile. Make sure you stand up straight and speak with confidence. All eyes are on you, so make sure your facial expressions match your tone.

Speak clearly and remember, the way you speak is just as important as what you are speaking about. Don't take 'no' or 'not interested' personally. You may have 50 people say no before you get 1 yes.

# WRITE YOUR ELEVATOR PITCH

Use what you have learned to write your elevator pitch. As your business idea develops, your pitch will change.

# Section 3 / THREE

# BRANDING & PROMOTIONS

# THE MARKETING PLAN

The Marketing Plan is part of a business plan. It outlines how you will advertise and market your business before and after you launch your business. It includes the marketing situation, your target markets, your goals, the strategies you will use to reach those goals, and how much it will all cost.

- *Marketing Situation*
  Includes description of your product/service, your advantages and disadvantages and threats from your competition.
- *Target Market*
  Who are your customers, where do they live, are they adults or children, how old are they etc.
- *Goals*
  Make the realistic and specific. Instead of saying I want to increase sales, you should say I will increase sales by 20%. It's also good to have a time frame to have the goal completed. are your customers, how old are they, where do they live, are they adults or children, how old are they etc.
- *Strategies*
  If your goal is to increase sales by 10%, you list all the ways you will do that. If you're selling candy apples 2 days a week, you could sell 2other days out of the week. You could also take orders online to be picked or delivered the next day. Also include the steps you'll use for letting customers know about the your new hours of operations and online ordering and delivery. Be thorough.
- *Budget*
  breakdown of the costs associated with each strategy. So if you plan to sell candy apple 2 additional days a week, you'll include the costs to make more candy apples. If the strategy you've chosen is too expensive (candy apple delivery would create the expense of additional insurance), you can revise your budget.

# THE FOUR P'S OF MARKETING
also known as the Marketing Mix

**01** **PRODUCT** - The product or service that meets a need or demand.

**02** **PRICE** - What your target market is willing to pay.

**03** **PROMOTION** - Persuading customers to buy your product or service.

**04** **PLACE** - Marketing to customers where they are (online, at events, at church etc.)

# TYPES OF MARKETING PROMOTION

Promotion is used to introduce new products and services to customers. It explains the benefits of buying the product or service, where or how to purchase it.

### Advertising
Businesses will pay for radio, newspaper, magazine, billboards & digital ads to get the word out about their product or service through *paid* ad placements.

### Promotional Sales
Businesses will discount their products or services for a short period of time to increase customer awareness and interest in their product or service.

### Direct Selling
Businesses have direct contact with their customers in person, through email, by phone or online. They may also give away samples, set up booths at events, or give sales presentations.

### Publicity
Sending information about a business, product, or service to the media to build the brand's image. Using influencers to introduce or endorse a product/service.

## THINGS TO KEEP IN MIND

# NAMING YOUR BUSINESS

 **BRAINSTORM IDEAS**

There are websites that help come up with company names, but you want your name and your brand to feel and be authenic as possible. Think about words that describe your product or service.

 **DO YOUR RESEARCH**

Google is a great place to start. You can also do a business search on the Secretary of State website and USPTO.gov to make sure your name does not already have a federally registered *trademark* or *service mark*.

 **DON'T LIMIT YOURSELF**

If you love your city or neighborhood, you may want to represent that in your business name, but customers outside those areas may feel excluded from your product.

 **K.I.S.S.**

Keep It Short & Simple. If people can't pronounce or spell your name, they will probably not use your product or service. If it's to hard to remember, you can miss out on a lot of word-of-mouth referrals.

 **DON'T MAKE IT TRENDY**

Trends come and go like seasons. The seasons always come back each year. A trend may not.

 **GET A SECOND OPINION**

Come up with several names and ask your family, friends, classmates, co-workers. You should also get feedback from your target market using market surveys.

# TM

## TRADEMARK

A SYMBOL, WORD, OR WORDS ESTABLISHED BY USE AS REPRESENTING A COMPANY OR *PRODUCT*. THE 'TM' SYMBOL ON A LOGO SHOWS THE COMPANY'S INTENT TO OBTAIN A REGISTERED TRADEMARK WITH THE US PATENT AND TRADEMARK OFFICE

## SERVICE MARK

A SYMBOL, WORD, OR WORDS ESTABLISHED BY USE AS REPRESENTING A COMPANY OR *SERVICE*. THE 'SM' SYMBOL ON A LOGO SHOWS THE COMPANY'S INTENT TO OBTAIN A REGISTERED TRADEMARK WITH THE US PATENT AND TRADEMARK OFFICE

# SM

## REGISTERED TRADEMARK

A SYMBOL, WORD, OR WORDS THAT IS A LEGALLY REGISTERED TRADEMARK WITH THE US PATENT AND TRADEMARK OFFICE ESTABLISHED BY USE AS REPRESENTING A COMPANY OR SERVICE.

# THE IMPORTANCE OF COLOR

### BLUE
*Trust, stability, dependability.*

### GREEN
*Health, growth, nature.*

### YELLOW
*Optimism, clarity warmth.*

### ORANGE
*Cheerful, friendly, fun.*

### BROWN
*Duty, endurance, stability.*

### RED
*Bold, Powerful, Youthful*

### PURPLE
*Exclusivity, Royalty, creativity*

### BLACK
*Sophistication, authority, power.*

### WHITE
*Clean, pure, simple.*

### DARK PINK
*Compassion, love nurturing*

'Research shows that the proper use of color increases brand recognition by 80%. It also raises the visual appearance by 93%. A further 85% of consumers buy because of color.'
Dena Przybyla - colorpsychology.org

# CREATE YOUR LOGO

Apply what you've learned and design two different concepts for your company's logo.

**CONCEPT 1**

# CREATE YOUR LOGO

Apply what you've learned and design two different concepts for your company's logo.

**CONCEPT 2**

# DESCRIBE YOUR LOGO

→ Use this worksheet to describe what your logo represents. What colors you chose, the design style and why.

_____

_____

_____

_____

_____

_____

_____

_____

_____

_____

_____

_____

_____

_____

_____

_____

_____

_____

# WRITE YOUR ELEVATOR PITCH

Use what you have learned to write your elevator pitch. As your business idea develops, your pitch will change.

# COST PER UNIT

You have to know the cost of making your product to properly price it. Add all your product expenses, then divide by the number of products you want to sell. This is your *cost per unit (CPU)*. In this example, we want to sell 100 caramel apples.

CPU = product expenses ÷ number of products you want to sell.

| | |
|---|---|
| 8lb can of caramel dip + 100 skewers | $45.99 |
| 108 granny smith apples | 52.68 (12 Bags x $4.39) |
| 50 pairs food grade disposable gloves | 4.29 |
| 100 candy apple bubbles | 14.58 |
| Product expenses | 117.54 |
| | |
| 117.54/100 candy apples = 1.1754 | 1.18 |

COST PER UNIT: $1.18

# Section 4

## FOUR

# PRICING

# COST FOR LABOR

You also add in the *cost for labor*. Determine an hourly rate, $15 for this example (based on industry specific, average hourly rate). Divide that by the number of caramel apples you can make in an hour, 8.
$15.00/8 = 1.875

COST FOR LABOR: $1.88

# COST OF DOING BUSINESS

Bizfluent.com defines the cost of doing business as all the expenses incurred by a firm or a sole proprietor in producing and selling goods or services. This includes licenses, permits, fees, internet, gas etc. For this example, we will only include costs for selling caramel apples at a festival.

| | |
|---|---:|
| Fair vendor fee (includes permits) | 50.00 |
| 2 Assistants ($25 each) | 50.00 |
| Gas | 10.00 |
| Total | 110.00 |
| $110.00/100 candy apples = | 1.10 |

OTHER EXPENSES:  1.10
COST PER UNIT:   1.18
COST FOR LABOR:  1.88

COST OF DOING BUSINESS:  $4.16

# MARKUP PRICING

*Markup in pricing* is the difference between the sell price and cost as a percentage. Many businesses use a 50% markup. This just means that they double their costs to set their sell price. Markup can be anywhere between 30% - 300%. For this example. we'll calculate using a 115% markup.

$4.66 * 115% = 5.5.359      $5.36

Add your cost of doing business to your markup price to get your sell price.

| | |
|---|---|
| cost of doing business | 4.16 |
| markup | 5.36 |
| **Sell Price** | **9.52** |

Once you set up at the event, you may change the sell price to match competitors, sell slightly above or below them, or price according to what your customers at the fair are willing to pay.

You may need certain permits & licenses before preparing & selling food. This xample is not a proposed business option and is used for instructional purposes only.

# PRICING
## YOUR SERVICE

### BUSINESS SUMMARY

**Pricing services is not as simple as pricing products.** To earn a profit on products, you sell the them for more than it cost to make. With services, you can charge a *flat rate*. This is the fee you charge no matter how large or small a job is. You can charge an hourly rate or give estimates on your services based on what the customer wants.

Let's say you mow lawns and charge $50 to mow the front and back. You can service 4 residences in one hour and make $200. Now, let's say you have a house with a huge front and back lawn and it takes you 1 hour to get the job done. You've made $50, but missed out on $150 because you weren't able to service 3 other customers in that hour.

The thing to remember is **you are trading your time for money**. The money you charge for your time is your *rate*. The rate is added to your cost to determine your price. The cost of equipment gas, fertilizer, herbicide, etc. You want to **make sure your price covers the cost of you providing your service.**

**Prices may vary based on customer needs.** In this example, a content creator is an online *freelancer* - someone who works as much or as little as they want.

This content creator offers 3 different pricing levels or *tiers for* different clients. The 1st tier is a basic plan for clients with small budgets or require minimal services. The 2nd tier is for clients wanting a combination of services and are willing to pay a bit more.

The 3rd tier is a premium client like a company wanting to create a themed event. Tier pricing helps the content creator reach more people.

Unless you work in a service industry that has regulated fees for service, you should never quote a flat fee without a client consultation.

### Consider the following when pricing your service:

- What are your *direct costs?* This includes things like supplies and *labor?*

- What are your *indirect costs?* Things like hiring a virtual assistant or advertising costs.

- What is your competition charging? Is your price above or below *market price?* Market research

- How much are your customers willing to pay? A *market study* or survey helps you find out.

There are service pricing calculators online to help you calculate direct and indirect costs, but it's wise to know how to price your services based on your skill and the amount of time and effort it takes to complete a project.

33

# PRICING

USE THIS SHEET TO PRICE YOUR PRODUCT OR SERVICE.

**BUSINESS SUMMARY**

# WRITE YOUR ELEVATOR PITCH

Use what you have learned to write your elevator pitch. As your business idea develops, your pitch will change.

# BUSINESS PLAN
## WRITING GUIDE

### WHAT IS A BUSINESS PLAN

A business plan is a written document that describes your idea for a product or service and how it will make money. It includes estimates for revenue, expenses, and how to make a profit. It will also include a marketing plan.

### WHY DO YOU NEED ONE

A business plan is like a blueprint to build your business. It forces you to look at every aspect of your business and shows investors that you are serious about your idea. The business plan worksheets you complete in this section gives you an idea of what goes into creating a business model. It does require some extra time, but it can keep you from making expensive mistakes later on.

### WHAT'S IN THE PLAN

- COVER PAGE
- TABLE OF CONTENTS
- EXECUTIVE SUMMARY
- COMPANY DESCRIPTION
- MARKET ANALYSIS
- COMPETITIVE ANALYSIS
- MANAGEMENT & ORGANIZATION
- PRODUCTS AND SERVICES
- MARKETING PLAN
- SALES STRATEGY
- REQUEST FOR FUNDING
- FINANCIAL PROJECTIONS

STARTUP   FUNDING   COST/UNIT

PRICE   PROFIT   STRATEGY

If you're trying to apply for a personal loan or a small business loan, you can always add an appendix or another section that provides additional financial or background information.

# BUSINESS PLAN
## WRITING GUIDE

## WHAT IS A BUSINESS PLAN

A business plan is a written document that describes your idea for a product or service and how it will make money. It includes estimates for revenue, expenses, and how to make a profit. It will also include a marketing plan.

## WHY DO YOU NEED ONE

A business plan is like a blueprint to build your business. It forces you to look at every aspect of your business and shows investors that you are serious about your idea. The business plan worksheets you complete in this section gives you an idea of what goes into creating a business model. It does require some extra time, but it can keep you from making expensive mistakes later on.

## WHAT'S IN THE PLAN

- COVER PAGE
- TABLE OF CONTENTS
- EXECUTIVE SUMMARY
- COMPANY DESCRIPTION
- MARKET ANALYSIS
- COMPETITIVE ANALYSIS
- MANAGEMENT & ORGANIZATION
- PRODUCTS AND SERVICES
- MARKETING PLAN
- SALES STRATEGY
- REQUEST FOR FUNDING
- FINANCIAL PROJECTIONS

STARTUP

FUNDING

COST/UNIT

PRICE

PROFIT

STRATEGY

> If you're trying to apply for a personal loan or a small business loan, you can always add an appendix or another section that provides additional financial or background information.

# BUSINESS PLAN
## COVER PAGE

### BUSINESS SUMMARY

This is an example of a business plan cover page. It includes your logo, the type of document it is, the business name, the business owner(s), business location, contact information, and a sentence describing your business. You may want to include the date so investors know exactly when the plan was written. Use an easy to read 12 point font and K.I.S.S.

**BUSINESS PLAN**

**PropertyRefs**

A Real Estate service company

Kendall & Rita Neal
Founder and CEO

**PROPERTYREFS, LLC**
1661  Suite 203F
Memphis, Tennessee 38115

901-690-2835
www.propertyrefs.com
propertyrefsofficial@gmail.com

# MY BUSINESS PLAN
## EXECUTIVE SUMMARY

## BUSINESS SUMMARY

Although it's the first page of your business plan, you should write the Executive Summary last. It is an overview of each section in your business plan. It should be no more than two pages long and be clear and concise. If you are seeking loans or investments, state how much you're looking for, and how you will use it.

_____
_____
_____
_____
_____
_____
_____
_____
_____
_____
_____
_____
_____
_____
_____
_____
_____
_____

# MY BUSINESS PLAN
## GENERAL DESCRIPTION

### BUSINESS SUMMARY

Tell a brief story about what made you want to start a business. Talk about your mission, goals and vision for your company.

_____
_____
_____
_____
_____
_____

Talk about your product or service and the industry. What is the problem it will solve? How is it different from what's available?

_____
_____
_____
_____

Summarize your business strategy here. What will you do to meet your goals? How are you going to make a profit?

_____
_____
_____
_____

# MY BUSINESS PLAN
## COMPETITIVE ADVANTAGE

BUSINESS SUMMARY

# Find Your Competitive Position with a SWOT Analysis

A S.W.O.T. Analysis is a study by a business to identify its internal strengths and weaknesses, as well as its external opportunities and threats. When comparing your business to competitors consider these key competitive factors: products, price, quality, selection, reputation, location, appearance, sales methods, advertising etc. These factors will differ across industries, so use factors relevant to your industry. Use

### Strengths

What advantages does your company have? What do you do better than anyone else? What are your unique selling points?

### Weaknesses

What areas can you improve on? What does your company lack? What things do your competitors do better than you?

### Opportunities

What changes in technology, policies, and social patterns can be a growth opportunity for the company?

### Threats

What are the obstacles to your company's growth? Who are your competitors? What changing factors can threaten your company's position?

# MY BUSINESS PLAN
## COMPETITIVE ANALYSIS

**BUSINESS SUMMARY**

STRENGTHS

_____
_____
_____

WEAKNESSES

_____
_____
_____

OPPORTUNITIES

_____
_____
_____

THREATS

_____
_____
_____

# MY BUSINESS PLAN
## MARKETING ANALYSIS

**BUSINESS SUMMARY**

Who are your customers? Adults, kids, moms, college students etc. Where do they live? How much money do they spend on your product or service?

_____
_____
_____
_____

Where will you sell your product or offer your service? At school, church, at a local festival or concert? Online?

_____
_____
_____
_____

How will you get the word out about your business? Social Media? Email? Hand out flyers? Radio or newspaper ads?

_____
_____
_____
_____

# MY BUSINESS PLAN
## MARKETING PLAN

### BUSINESS SUMMARY

How big is your target market? Be as detailed as possible. Give statistics and sources.

_____
_____
_____
_____
_____
_____

Explain how you will price your products and if there will be service fees (registration, returned item, late fees)?

_____
_____
_____
_____
_____
_____

# MY BUSINESS PLAN
## MANAGEMENT AND ORGANIZATION

Investors and lenders want to know about your employees, their skill sets. List job descriptions, job requirements and training, and your standard operating procedures. Will you have contract workers? 1099 employees?

## Owners and Key Personnel

As owner, will you run day to day operations or will you hire a manager? If you will have 10 or more employees you'll need an organizational that outlines who is responsible for what for key functions. If you're applying for loans or seeking investors, include resumes of owners and key employees. If applicable, list board of directors, advisory board, attorney, accountant. insurance agent, banker, consultants, or mentors. You'll also need to provide personal financial statements for owners and any major stockholders.

For business plan templates and more go to:
https://www.score.org/search/site/templates

## ➡ Production

How are your services produced? Where are your services produced? Explain how much it costs to produce your product or provide your service, Elaborate on your methods for ensuring quality, customer service, inventory control and product development. Discuss the business location, how big it is, the type of building, zoning, power and other utilities needed, rent, insurance - everything associated with producing your product or providing your service.

## ➡ Inventory

Keep an accurate count of the kind of inventory you have like supplies or finished goods. Also includes things like order and delivery costs. This section should also list suppliers that are key to opeations. List the business name and address, the kind of inventory provided, how much, their credit and delivery policies. You may also in list any back up suppliers in the evnt of a shortage. Talk about cost of supplies and how you deal with fluctuating costs. If you plan to issue credit (30 days same as credit.

## ➡ Legal

This section lets the investor or loan officer know that your business is a legal entity, compliant with all local, state, and federal requirements. If you have a a service based busniess, do you have to meet any licensing or bonding requirements?What permits will you need? What are the zoning or building code requirements? Do you have business insurance? Are you in compliance with health, workplace or environmental regulations? Work with an attorney or industry profess ional familiar with the legalities of the idustry you're working

# MY BUSINESS PLAN
## STARTUP COSTS

### BUSINESS SUMMARY

How much will you need to start your business? What do you need to buy before you can get started? How much will everything cost? The amount of money you need to launch your business is called the "startup cost".

_____
_____
_____
_____

Where will you get the money to cover your startup costs? Are you getting a loan from a family member? Taking money out of your savings account?

_____
_____
_____
_____

How much will you charge? How does your pricing compare to your competitors? Make sure you set your price above the cost per unit.

_____
_____
_____
_____

# MY BUSINESS PLAN
## FINANCE

## BUSINESS SUMMARY

How much will you make on each sale after you subtract your expenses? This is your profit.  Profit = Income - Expenses

**Sell Price:**
_____

**Cost of Item:**
_____

**Profit:**
_____

_____

_____

_____

_____

How much will you make in a month? 12 months? The financial analysis section of your business plan will show your potential earnings over a 5 year period. You will need the help of an accountant to help prepare your *financial projection*. A financial projection is a forecast of future revenues and expenses.

_____

_____

_____

_____

_____

_____

_____

# WRITE YOUR ELEVATOR PITCH

Use what you have learned to write your elevator pitch. As your business idea develops, your pitch will change.

# FOR MORE INFO AND BUSINESS RESOURCES

## US SMALL BUSINESS ADMINISTRATION

- PROCUREMENT TECHNICAL ASSISTANCE CENTER
- VETERANS BUSINESS OUTREACH CENTER
- SMALL BUSINESS DEVELOPMENT CENTER
- U.S. EXPORT ASSISTANCE CENTER
- WOMEN'S BUSINESS CENTER
- SCORE BUSINESS MENTOR

  WWW.SBA.GOV

## CHAMBER OF COMMERCE

WWW.USCHAMBER.COM

# DEFINITIONS

**Advertising** – the activity or profession of producing advertisements for commercial products or services.

**Brainstorming** - group discussion to produce ideas or solve problems.

**Branding** - distinctive wording or design used to identify a particular brand.

**Consumer** - a person who purchases goods and services for personal use.

**Cost per unit** - a measure of a company's cost to build or create one unit of product. Divide the total manufacturing costs by the number of items produced to arrive at the production

**Direct cost** - An expense such as for labor, material, fuel or power that can be traced directly to a service or product.

**Direct selling** - Face to face presentation, demonstration, and sale of products or services, usually at the home or office of a prospect

**Entrepreneurship** - the activity of setting up a business or businesses, taking on financial risks in the hope of profit.

**Flat rate** - a rate that is the same for everyone no matter how big or small a job is.

**Ideation** - the formation of ideas or concepts.

**Indirect costs** - Expenses like storage or maintenance that indirectly affect your cost.

**Logo** - a symbol or other design adopted by an organization to identify its products, uniform, vehicles, etc.

# DEFINITIONS

**Market research -** the action or activity of gathering information about consumers needs and preferences.

Marketing - the action or business of promoting and selling products or services, including market research and advertising.

**Markup in price -** the difference between a product's selling price and cost as a percentage of the cost.

**Persuasive advertising** - a type of product promotion that aims to persuade a consumer for buying a particular product, especially
in the presence of several similar products in the same category.

**Pivot** - Helps a business recover from a tough period, or survive after experiencing new competition or other factors that make the original business model unsustainable.

**Profit** - a financial gain, especially the difference between the
amount earned and the amount spent in buying, operating, or producing something.

**Projections - e**stimates of the future financial performance of a business.

**Promotional sales** - stimulation of sales achieved through contests, demonstrations, discounts, exhibitions or trade shows, games, giveaways, point-of-sale displays and merchandising, special offers, and similar activities.

**Promotions** - to publicize a product, organization, or venture so as to increase sales or public awareness.

**Publicity** - the giving out of information about a product, person, or
company for advertising or promotional purposes.

# DEFINITIONS

**Revenue -** the total amount of income generated by the sale of goods or services related to the business primary operations.

**Registered trademark -** a distinctive mark or symbol to which a person or company has declared ownership by filing the trademark with the US Patent and Trademark Office.

**Sell price** - price at which a product or service is sold to the buyer.

**Service mark** - a symbol, word, or words legally registered or established by use as representing a company or service.

**Startup cost** - Non-recurring costs associated with setting up business, such as accountant's fees, legal fees, registration charges, as well as advertising, promotional activities.

**Target market** - a particular group of consumers at which a product or service is aimed.

**Trademark** - a symbol, word, or words legally registered or established by use as representing a company or product.

**Unique selling point** - The factor or consideration presented by a seller as the reason that one product or service is different from and better than that of the competition.

# REFERENCES

https://www.amazon.com/

https://www.bizfluent.com

https://www.colorpsychology.org/color-psychology-marketing/

https://www.corporatefinanceinstitute.com

https://datavizcatalogue.com/methods/brainstorm.html

https://designthinking.ideo.com/

https://www.entrepreneur.com/encyclopedia

www.forbes.com

https://www.investopedia.com/terms/f/four-ps.asp

https://www.investopedia.com/financial-edge/1010/top-6-reasons-new-businesses-fail.aspx

https://www.lexico.com/en/definition

https://www.national.biz/2019-small-business-failure-rate-startup-statistics-industry/

# REFERENCES

https://www.officedepot.com/cm/article/4-components-of-the-perfect-elevator-pitch

https://www.profolus.com/topics/types-of-promotion-in-marketing/

https://www.sba.gov/media/training/encore_09012016/story_content/external_files/Readiness%20Assessment.pdf

https://www.score.org/resource/business-plan-template-startup-business

https://www.uspto.gov/trademarks-getting-started/trademark-basics/trademark-patent-or-copyright

# WORKBOOK OF BUSINESS SERIES

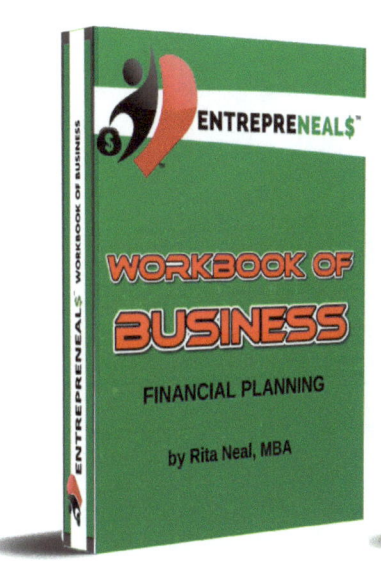

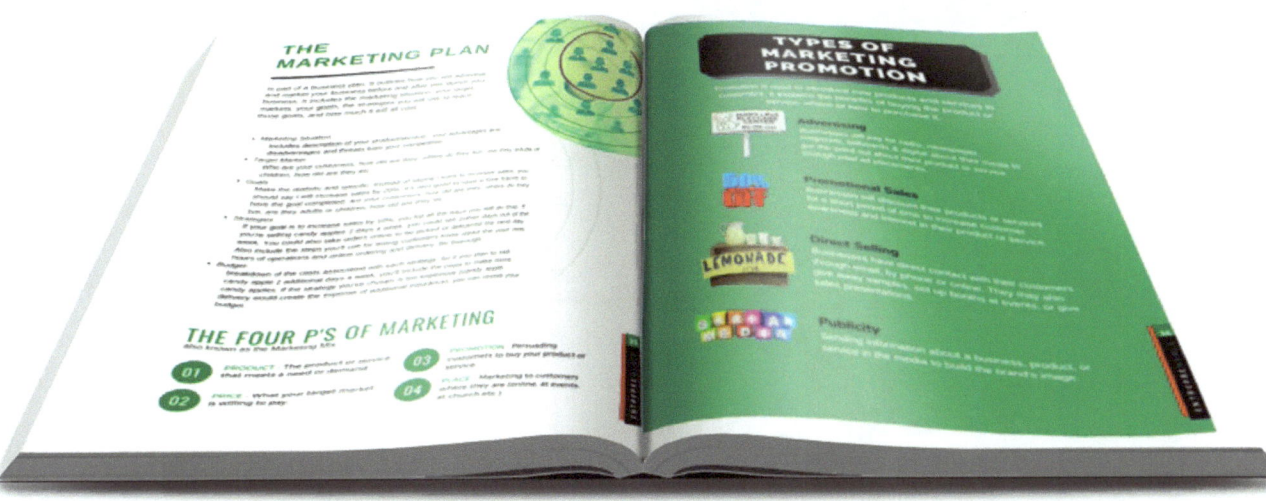

# DIRECT DEPOSIT *GONE* BEFORE YOU GET IT?

## LIVING IN YOUR OVERDRAFT!

**LEARN HOW TO:**
- Manage your money relationship
- Keep more of what you earn

**6-WEEK MONEY MINDSET INTENSIVE**

- MINDSET MAKEOVER
- BORROW, LOAN, SPEND GUIDE
- REALISTIC BUDGET BLUEPRINT
- SAVINGS SCAVENGER HUNT
- MONEY MOVES
- LEGACY BUILDING

## WWW.ENTREPRENEALS.COM

www.ingramcontent.com/pod-product-compliance
Lightning Source LLC
Chambersburg PA
CBHW042026150426
43198CB00002B/76